Harmony at Home: A Guide to African Family Life

Stanley Mwadzama

Published by Stanley Mwadzama, 2024.

HARMONY AT HOME: A GUIDE TO AFRICAN FAMILY LIFE

First edition. December 22, 2024.

ISBN: 979-8230365938

Written by Stanley Mwadzama.

Also by Stanley Mwadzama

Harmony at Home: A Guide to African Family Life

Table of Contents

To the innumerable families in Africa who work tirelessly every day to create cozy, resilient, and peaceful homes.

To my dear wife, whose strength, love, and support have been my compass on this journey.

And may this book serve as a guide and a reminder to future generations that the ties we forge and the customs we treasure are what make us strong.

With admiration and optimism.

"A family is the compass that directs us; it is strong because it is nourished by the promise of the future and has roots in tradition. Family comes first, no matter what.

Introduction

The close proximity of family in the African home explains how important personal space is to Africans. Therefore, finally, every home in Africa encompasses a mixture of tradition and modernity, a mixture of discipline and love, and a mixture of belonging and understanding. As the nation evolves, so too do the challenges that African families face in seeking peace. So then, how do we build strong families that keep our culture alive and are able to meet the challenges of the 21st century? The book, Harmony at Home, attempts to respond to this by providing guidance on how African families can be built and maintained so that they are not only healthy but able to succeed despite the challenges that the world faces at this time.

For many generations, the family has been the focal point for African society, providing power, sustenance, and self. But many families are now grappling with issues related to urbanization, globalization, and technology. These are all things that have transformed how we live as families, often in ways that make it difficult to create the kinds of families we want to have. This book recognizes the unique obstacles faced by African families and offers strategies for navigating these turbulent waters. It employs both traditional wisdom and modern research to formulate practical, culturally appropriate solutions.

In "Harmony at Home," all aspects of family life are seen through the lens of family well-being in Africa. This book doesn't just draw on Western notions about how families ought to function. Instead, it recognizes African families living in unique cultural contexts and offers tools built from our culture, weaved with our stories and beliefs. The lessons in each part are as relevant to African life, such as how to talk to your spouse better or how to manage your work and family life.

As it stands now, there are a lot of good high points in the book that are good for family peace for Africans. But the most essential thing is to communicate with one another. Though people in this region often use body language as indirect communication (the book discusses how to have good conversations between spouses, parents and children, and extended family members, for example), the tables and chairs are close and the shapes of spaces are well-defined. It offers helpful advice on how to actively listen, discuss feelings, and resolve disagreements in ways that build up rather than drive apart family bonds.

The second key theme is the difficulty of reconciling tradition with technology. African cultures, too, are shifting rapidly, and many families find themselves at war between preserving love over their old traditions and coming to terms with new realities. This book offers guidance in finding the right balance between following old rites and embracing new doctrines. It's about how to hold a family together in a world in which people are becoming increasingly self-focused and also about combining old and new ways of parenting.

It also covers another important topic—money management. With many different family situations on the continent, the book also offers tailored budgeting, saving, and investing advice that factors in how the African economy functions. It also mentions kids using money and the problem of how to educate them so the next generation is financially free and rich; not many will talk about it.

It's a book about the extended family, which is fitting because aunts and uncles and grandparents and cousins play such a large part in African family life. This style of relationship can be very useful and make people happy, but it can also be difficult to manage and lead to conflicts. "Harmony at Home," there are realistic approaches to maintaining strong family ties with extended family members while keeping healthy limits and expectations in check.

Lastly, the book instills emotional intelligence and gets family members to feel emotionally close. In a culture where the Swiss hold on tight and letting it all out is frowned on, this book tells how to make your home a space of loving connection and respect where everyone feels supported, understood, and cared for. It searches for cultural clues about how, for example, we express love, grow closer to a partner over time, or raise our children to be emotionally resilient.

"Harmony at Home" is for African readers, acknowledging that we have cousin bonds but that our family systems and cultural practices are significantly varied. This book has advice and inspiration that can help you have an engaging relationship, whether you're a newlywed couple starting off, parents struggling to raise kids in a fast-changing world, or an older person wanting to meaningfully engage with younger people.

The book offers young couples a blueprint for building a family that will endure for a century. The book provides guidance on communication, problem-solving, and financial matters, areas that have the potential to significantly impact a marriage, yet often fall short in traditional premarital counseling. It also describes the stresses faced by young African couples, for example, weighing career aspirations against family responsibilities and coping with in-laws.

Parents can find a wealth of advice on raising children who either feel ashamed of their culture or are proud of their origins, yet feel at ease in any part of the world. You will discover the best way to raise your child, how to raise them to be responsible and independent, and how to manage the issues that arise from being an African parent in our current day. To clarify, turn it into: This book also shows you how to speak to children about tough topics, including sex, money, and national identity.

"Harmony at Home" also demonstrates to people in the "sandwich generation," who are caring for both aging parents and children, how to navigate their professional and personal lives while maintaining their own health and happiness. It addresses topics such as how to manage the expectations of extended family, how to cope with financial stress, and how to find time to take care of yourself when everyone else is demanding your undivided attention.

We provided the skills and knowledge that older people and grandparents need to participate in family life in the modern world. The book offers plenty of tips on how to navigate age gaps, impart what you know in a way that younger family members can take in, and make the most of how your family dynamics are evolving.

In this book, readers are equipped with all the tools they need in order to build and maintain healthy, resilient families. For the first time in their lives, they'll learn how to use communication instead of fighting, how to address disagreements quietly, how to manage the finances properly, and how to turn the family wounds into positivity. It offers couples advice on how to address some of the most frequent challenges they encounter, such as infidelity, navigating in-laws, and work-life balance. It provides hope and practical solutions, even for the most challenging family issues.

This book is also a cultural history that will help its readers better understand the forces at work in African family life today. Here, the book guides us on how best to hold on to our heritage as we navigate the newness of the modern technology age and the accepting of the old and new within Africa. Through this, they can have a better understanding of the other person and possibly deepen empathy and understanding.

What matters most is that "Harmony at Home" provides people with the tools they need to become active co-creators of the future of their family. Individuals will discover how not only to manage the stresses of modern life but also to make their family life what they want it to be. They will know how to be deliberate with their family traditions, values, and goals, and they will have the tools to do that.

Read on and discover new ways to think and act. Thank you for joining us here on "Harmony at Home," where every task is an opportunity for growth! It's not always easy, but it's always worth it. If you are looking to strengthen family ties or mend broken... It offers steadfast advice and beneficial direction for creating a home filled with love, respect, and understanding.

In the upcoming pages, we will delve into the fundamentals of family unity. We will be discussing everything from creating a healthy family dynamic to navigating life's challenges as a family. Using real-life examples and the latest studies, we will discuss the good and the bad aspects of African family life by providing you with practical tools and flagship recommendations.

You'll discover how to transform your home life into a sanctuary for growth and contemplation for you and your family. "Together we'll get through the tough stuff of talking to your spouse, showing you how to express your needs, listening with empathy, and coming to a healthy resolution for you both." You'll discover how to be a purposeful parent for life, how to combine love and discipline to teach your child African values, and prepare him/her to be a member of the world.

We'll discuss the topic so many dread when it comes to the holidays: extended family—how to manage tricky relationships with in-laws and other cousins and how to establish healthy boundaries. We equip you with your tools to manage your resources, create wealth over time, and be able to pass on wealth to your family by teaching real-world financial literacy in Africa. We are going to discuss a few of the issues experienced by many African families that don't get a lot of airtime, such as cheating, fear, infertility, and everything in between. They teach you how to create emotional connections that keep love and desire alive even in long-term relationships. When issues arise (and they always do), you will have the skills to navigate those challenges together and emerge even stronger and more connected than before.

This does what the first did—building on that to give you a complete plan for driving peace to your own family. Every lesson and experience you gain from one aspect of family life enhances your overall performance. This will create a virtuous cycle of learning, sharing, and love.

But "Harmony at Home" is more than a book; it's a call to action. As you interpret, contemplate, and apply the concepts within these pages, you will embark on a road of development and discovery. You'll be asked to meditate on what you think family is, to release patterns of behavior that don't serve you anymore, and to consider fresh ways to handle your most important relationships.

This won't always be a smooth road to drive on. If this is going to translate into true unity at home, you have to

Be courageous, dedicated, and curious." But the payoffs are difficult to quantify. The only way out is to achieve that perfect home, where people can laugh at ease, where fights can be solved with grace, and where all understanding can flow like water.

We guide young people to discover who they are and what they want to do in the world. This prepares them for marriage, itself a journey that improves over time as two people unite in love and intention as equals.

That's the ideal that "Harmony at Home" wants you to achieve. This is the resource you need to become that person fast—whether you're just starting to create a family or looking for ways to breathe new life into the lifetime relationships you've already built." Now, open your heart and mind to the possibilities presented in Chapter 1. Prepare to grow, laugh, and cry. While fostering a peaceful family life may seem challenging, this book provides guidance on how to achieve it!

Glad to be here at "Harmony at Home." Allow the change to happen.

Chapter 1: The Foundation of Family Harmony

Understanding the importance of family in African culture

In African countries, family is more than just a group of related individuals; it forms the foundation of your society, your identity, and your cultural layer. The concept of family in Africa is broad and far-reaching, extending well beyond the nuclear family familiar to many in the West. It derives from distant cousins, ancestors, and even unborn children. This larger view of family is rooted in the African philosophy and worldview, in which everything is interconnected and everyone is accountable to one another.

In African society, you cannot overemphasize the value of family! It's the primary avenue by which people receive social support, collaborate on business problems, and seek moral counsel. However, from birth through death, a human being is inextricably tied into the web of familial relationships that begins to define their obligation, connection, and meaning. As the great African philosopher John S. Mbiti once said, "I am because we are, and since we are therefore I am." This profound statement captures the core of African family philosophy: that families on the continent rely on each other and support each other.

In many African cultures, the family is a sacred organization that is overseen by spiritual forces and blessed by ancestors. This spiritual aspect lends more depth and respect to family ties, and it is part of what helps past, present, and future generations feel connected. The family is often seen as a microcosm of the overall community, where every person is very important for maintaining the peace and balance of the whole.

In Africa, when we talk of family, we mean the entire community, and blood relatives are often indistinguishable from the other people in your community. People often call each other by terms that signify family relations (e.g., brother, sister, aunt, uncle) even when those people are not blood relatives. This stems from the deep-rooted sense of family and duty inherent in African society. Such a wide view of family creates a strong sense of community and social connectedness, allowing individuals to tap into an enormous web of resources and support.

Fundamental aspects of a healthy family life

IN AFRICA, A GOOD FAMILY dynamic consists of some key factors that work together to create harmony for family members and their environment. These are common in many ways but expressed very differently in African culture.

Order and respect are big things in African families. The older generation are often those who are respected and whose knowledge and experience are considered so critical to the well-being of the clan. Thanks to this respect for age and experience, a natural hierarchy exists in the family, and everyone knows their job and responsibilities. But it should be borne in mind that this order is not meant to be repressive. Rather, it's designed to help people make decisions and resolve their differences.

A good family dynamic is also about good communication. In African families, communication is typically not just about the words we use. When family members speak openly and honestly with each other, they understand each other better, care about each other, and connect with each other. It enables individuals to express their desires, needs, and concerns, thereby ensuring that everyone within the system feels heard and appreciated.

In Africa, family life is about support and togetherness. One translation of the idea of "ubuntu" is "I am, because we are" to emphasize how family members are connected and must support one another. This unity manifests itself in many ways, from contributing financially when someone needs it to uplifting them emotionally when life goes south. It creates a safety net that protects and grounds the whole family.

The ability to change and shift is becoming a more vital part of modern African homes. Families will need to adapt their structures and rituals to the changing society and new issues while retaining their fundamental values. Perhaps it's a balance between keeping family and spending time together that's traditional as opposed to something that's that new and has yet to be seen or a new way to stay connected with family as the cities grow or the world shrinks.

This is a vital aspect of ensuring that every member of the family stays healthy. Every culture might have its own way of showing affection; however, all of us seek mental support and affirmation. Healthy African families strike a balance between maintaining traditional hierarchy and respect and emotional intimacy with one another.

Ideating common goals and values for your family

ESTABLISHING SHARED beliefs and objectives is an important component of contributing to the family becoming a peaceful environment. When this occurs in Africa, the result is often a blending of traditional cultural values and modern goals to create a unique family philosophy that guides behavior and decisions.

Establishing shared beliefs and goals should be a collective effort that engages everyone in the family in age-appropriate ways. This transparency ensures that everybody in the family has an interest in its future and desires its success. It can be in the form of family meetings, formal or informal, depending on the style and culture of the family.

When you set goals, it helps to consider both short-term and long-term ends. Long-term goals are also acceptable, such as finding a way to enjoy better with others or achieving some family traditions or goals. These long-term goals might involve plans for education, a career, or the entire family long after you (and the baby) have gone. These goals should be SMART: specific, measurable, achievable, relevant, and time-bound. It will point the family in a direction and give them impetus.

Values, by contrast, are the principles that guide how the family approaches decision-making and behavior. These include respecting elders, going to school, working hard, being kind to others, and upholding cultural practices—things that African families often instill in their children. Of course, each family will have its own set of values rooted in their experiences, beliefs, and aspirations.

Such shared beliefs and goals have to be examined and reevaluated. Goals and objectives should evolve as families change and grow. Having that conversation regularly and often keeps the family aligned and committed to the purpose.

Creating a supportive and nurturing home environment

FAMILY HARMONY THRIVES best in a home in which everyone feels supported and cared for. This context encompasses the entire house and much more in Africa. It also encompasses the spiritual, emotional, and social aspects of family life.

It takes up a lot of physical space to create a nurturing atmosphere. Traditional African architecture often reflected the way families collect together as a group, with rooms that were designed to enable interaction and functionality for people to interact and do things together. Even though housing has changed since then, creating environments that can bring families closer together remains a goal. That might mean reserving spaces for family gatherings, ensuring that communal areas are warm and inviting, and incorporating African art and design to foster a sense of cultural connectedness.

One really important part of a caring home is supporting each other emotionally. That means ensuring everyone in the family feels safe to express their feelings, share their anxiety, and ask for help when they need it. You have to be able to listen, comprehend, and validate what each of you is experiencing and feeling. In Africa, the crocodile's strength lies in the water. Just like the strength of a family lies in being able to provide mental support to its members.

In African families, spiritual growth is a core component of daily life. Many of the continent's families take strength and direction from their faith, be it through formal religious observance or more traditional spiritual outlooks. Having a place in the home for spiritual growth and expression can help to add a level of caring to the home. It can include having regular prayer times, discussing moral and ethical issues, or participating in religious or cultural practices.

Intellectual stimulation is another key component of a supportive home environment. Fostering interests, critical thinking, and lifelong learning can improve family life and benefit everyone. That may include talking regularly about current events, reading and discussing the same books, or doing educational activities together as a family.

Families from Africa need to be connected to their culture for their homes to be safe. It is about actively protecting and celebrating cultural heritage through language, food, music, stories, and customs. Kwame Gyekye, a psychologist who specializes in African culture in Ghana, said: "Culture is not static; society is dynamic; the environment is changing all the time. Help between family members to balance tradition and beliefs with modern life is also needed to keep cultural connections alive.

Therefore, it is advantageous to establish connections with other residents in order to improve family relationships. Part of that involves taking time to share experiences, whether it's family meals, game nights, group projects, or just hanging out and spending time together. These shared experiences allow family members to feel rooted together, remember each other, and ultimately grow closer (emotionally or socially) with time.

Routine/Consistency & Security

A SENSE OF SECURITY and stability can be established within the home through routine and consistency. While flexibility is key, as so many things in family life are unpredictable, having a few things that happen regardless can help ground matters down and act as anchors of sorts amidst the chaos. This might mean returning to normal family zoning-out meetings, meal times, or bedtimes to show the person that life—without their absence—continues, we may need to reject our own grief spiral.

A home where there is support must have clear ways to communicate with each other. That doesn't just mean getting people to talk, but listening to their body language and ensuring people feel secure enough to have difficult conversations without fearing judgment or retribution. "The single story creates stereotypes," the Nigerian author Chimamanda Ngozi Adichie said. "The trouble with stereotypes is not that they are untrue, but that they are partial. By encouraging open discussion, everyone in the family can express their ideas and experiences.

Each small win should be acknowledged and celebrated. This is part of creating an environment of care. This helps the family members build self-esteem and motivation, which tends to make them pursue their goals and aspirations. Celebrate not just academic or work success, but growth as a person, acts of kindness, and struggles to get through difficult times.

Resolving conflicts is another key aspect of maintaining a comfortable and safe atmosphere in your home. Each and every family has issues and disputes, but these issues are appropriately addressed in a nurturing house by focusing on understanding, compromising, and enacting solutions that work for the whole family. Teaching and practicing healthy ways to resolve conflicts can help family life be a lot more peaceful.

Creating a home where everyone feels secure, both physically and emotionally, is crucial. And that means not only keeping them physically safe, but keeping them emotionally safe, if you will, not abusing them, neglecting them, or criticizing them too harshly. It's about ensuring that everyone in the family has a safe, respectful, valued—and valued—place.

Flexibility and adaptability are key components of a loving home environment, and they help when unexpected life events or problems come up. For the sake of long-term family harmony, you'll need the ability to adjust family dynamics, routines, or standards as necessary without straying from core values and goals.

In conclusion, the making of a safe and caring home in Africa encompasses the Moonshot-based approach of meeting every single one of a person's basic needs, including physical, mental, spiritual, intellectual, and social. It takes effort, communication, and commitment to create an environment of love, respect, and growth. Building this environment becomes a process of family development and style rather than a goal as families navigate life's superficial demands while preserving their cultural legacy.

Chapter 2: Mastering the Art of Marital Communication

Continuing the overview of the basics of family unity from the last chapter, this one will discuss one of the most essential parts of a happy marriage—communication. As with relationships anywhere in the world, good conversation is the foundation upon which African marriages are built. This field elaborates extensively on ways to get through to your partner, offering advice and possibilities designed for African couples' cultural contexts.

Techniques for couples to use active listening

Active listening is a very important skill for couples who want to communicate well but is often overlooked. Many couples listen to what the other person says but fail to truly listen, resulting in misunderstandings and conflicts that do not get resolved. Active listening requires you to fully engage with your partner's words, feelings, and underlying messages instead of just hearing what they have to say. Part of active listening is the art of reflective listening.

To do so, you should paraphrase what your partner said to confirm you understood it correctly. For example, your wife might complain that she has to do cleaning, and then you could say, "It sounds like you feel overwhelmed about the volume of work and could use more help." Is that right?" Not only does this method demonstrate that you're paying attention, but it also gives you the opportunity to clarify if something is unclear.

The other core aspect of active listening is sustaining eye contact and exhibiting behavioral signs that you're paying attention. Straight for the eyes is a sign of respect and care in many African cultures. But you should also be mindful of cultural differences; prolonged eye contact or staring, for example, can be perceived as rude or hostile in some communities. Adapt your communication with the partner to accommodate their culture while allowing them to feel listened to and valued. When engaging in active listening, it is also important not to break in.

Despite your inclination to interrupt and add your own thoughts, strive to listen attentively and fully understand their perspective before making any suggestions or ideas. Nigerian author Chimamanda Ngozi Adichie once said, "The single story creates stereotypes, and the problem with stereotypes is not that they are untrue, but that they are incomplete. By hearing your partner's full side of the story, you can get a clearer picture of what they are thinking and feeling.

Communicating needs and feelings clearly

Using effective communication and being able to convey your words to your partner can also help to reach a middle ground, the so-called win-win, whenever situations occur and controversy happens in the relationship. In many African cultures, especially among men, stoicism is a trait that is highly valued. In Malawi, there is a saying that goes, "Banja mkupirira" (Marriage is endurance). This can make it challenging to express your feelings. But in order for a marriage to work, both people need to feel safe discussing their wants and needs.

This is when using "I" statements is a good way to express your wants. Telling someone, "You never help around the house," can come off as accusatory and put the other person on the defensive. Instead, say, "I can't do all the chores alone." "In this area, I require more assistance." This approach does not accuse your partner but instead addresses your needs and feelings. This will increase your chances of getting the response from your partner that you would like.

It's also always important to be really forthright about how you feel and what you desire. Giving your partner vague explanations, such as "I'm not happy," doesn't help them to understand your feelings. Instead, work to find where your feelings originate and name them. For example, you might say, "I feel disconnected from you because we haven't spent real time together in weeks." How about we can have one evening spent together in a week?

Timing is yet another component of any clear communication. When it comes to discussing something important, timing can influence the success of your message. Avoid discussing sensitive matters when both of you are tired, stressed, or in a rush. Instead, schedule important conversations for a time when you're both calm and can focus on each other.

Breaking down communication barriers

MESSY COMMUNICATION habits—even among well-meaning couples—can lead to problems. Culture and social norms can make those problems particularly strong in African marriages. It makes for better conversation in a marriage to acknowledge and confront these issues.

A common barrier is the fear of being left open to attack. In several African societies, especially with men, being open and vulnerable is regarded as a weakness There is a Malawian proverb that says "Mwamuna salira" (A real man does not cry). Due to this cultural expectation, it can be difficult for couples to discuss their greatest fears and emotions.

Getting through this block requires a concerted effort to create a safe, judgment-free space in the relationship where each party feels safe to be open and vulnerable.

Another huge issue is how gender roles influence how people speak to each other. In many African countries, traditional gender roles can dictate how men and women speak with one another. For example, women may not have the right to openly tell their husbands that they disagree with them, while men never feel they can look anything but strong and in control. If you want to shift these knee-jerk patterns, you have to be willing to name them and reevaluate and iterate on cultural norms so they serve your relationship.

There may also be a language barrier in areas with lots of different languages spoken between several different racial groups. Even couples who share the same language may struggle to understand each other completely due to minor shifts in dialect or new cultural idioms. In order to address these language barriers, the people around the individual need to take the time to ensure they understand and request clarifications when things are unclear.

Issues outside the marriage, such as extended family members or the community's expectations, can also cause spouses to struggle to communicate openly with each other. In much of Africa, marriage is not just between two people but two families. This can be an excellent way to receive support, but it can also make it difficult for the couples to communicate with each other. To overcome this hurdle, it's crucial to establish firm boundaries with extended family members and prioritize direct communication between spouses.

African perspectives on non-verbal communication

WORDS MATTER IN A MARRIAGE, but nonverbal communication is also very powerful and often conveys messages clearer than words alone. African cultures particularly focus on nonverbal communication, which is a highly complex and subtle social skill, as this form of communication reflects profound cultural values and norms.

"Everyone uses facial expressions to communicate without words, but the way they're understood can vary based on society. In a lot of African cultures, maintaining a neutral expression in important discussions is a sign of respect and engagement. A partner of a different ethnic background may, however, interpret this as a lack of interest or empathy. Understanding these cultural differences in facial expressions and talking about them can help clear up that confusion and improve communication overall.

Another key component of nonverbal communication is body language. In a lot of African countries, we show love and support by being close and touching each other. Well, the right amount of physical contact can vary tremendously, depending on the culture and the context. For example, in more conservative neighborhoods, PDAs (public displays of affection) between couples might be considered rude. For nonverbal conversation to succeed, you both need to be mindful of these cultural standards and determine what is pleasant for you both.

Some African cultures place great emphasis on the use of silence in conversation. In some Western contexts, silence may seem awkward or a sign of having difficulty communicating. But in many African societies, comfortable silence is revered and can convey profound understanding or reverence. Learning when and how to appreciate and utilize silence as a form of communication can enhance conversation in a marriage and deepen emotional bonds.

In several African countries, even posture and how one moves both one's hands can have profound implications when another word isn't being spoken. For example, it is considered extremely rude in many West African cultures to point to someone with your finger. In some East African cultures, crossing one leg over the other at the knees while seated in front of leaders or those in power is considered rude. Understanding these cultural differences and discussing how they impact your relationship can help you steer clear of offending each other unintentionally and enhance communication.

Though volume and tone of voice are components of spoken language, they convey meaningful nonverbal messages that can have a tremendous impact on the messages that are being sent. In many African countries, speaking softly denotes respect and control, while higher volume can indicate loss of control and disrespect. However, these interpretations can lead to significant differences across different locations and ethnic groups. To ensure that their words are understood correctly, couples should communicate about the personal and cultural meanings associated with different tones and volumes. From the outset of this discussion on communication in a marriage, it's evident that while some individuals may effortlessly navigate the learning curve; mastering it requires time, cultural awareness, and practice. It's important to remember that hearing, accepting, and checking in with one another can also require tenderness, which is the willingness to change and grow alongside one another. These are the skills and strategies in this chapter that will improve communication in your African marriage. But they need to be employed regularly and in a way suited to each couple's situation and culture.

Sharing knowledge is not enough if you are also an excellent communicator; you have to understand, empathize, and build a deeper emotional intimacy between two people. Wole Soyinka | the profoundest threat to the act of freedom is that you cannot criticize it. This gives us the very important lesson that honest, open, and polite communication is suitable for both partners' growth and freedom when we think about marriage. In this, you can give and accept constructive comments.

And remember, as we move to our next chapter, which will be how to deal with conflicts with grace, the communications skills we've covered are the most essential skills when it comes to conflict management. If you work on listening well, communicating clearly, overcoming communication barriers, and reading body language, you will be better equipped to handle the disagreements and issues that are bound to crop up in a marriage. Improving communication in a marriage takes time and effort, but with persistence, practice, and a mutual goal, it is too possible to create a sturdier, more enjoyable relationship.

Chapter 3: Navigating Conflicts with Grace

Now that we covered how to communicate with your spouse, let's cover another integral aspect of family harmony: how to resolve disagreements. African weddings, like any other type of relationship, have their own share of arguments. The health and longevity of our unions are dependent on the ways we contend with and resolve these differences.

The factors that cause conflict in all marriages.

HOW FAMILY, CULTURAL values and expectations, and individual differences interact to produce African marriage problems. Disagreement is mainly a consequence of old versus new standards. There are several other causes of disagreement, but the old versus new standards dilemma is one of the major ones. With African cultures rapidly modernizing, couples struggle to preserve ancient traditions while accepting new mores.

For instance, the role of women in marriage is a major point of contention in many African households. Women were once supposed to be modest and devote most of their energies to housework. But as women achieve greater education and employment opportunities, a large portion now desire equal partnerships, in which they make decisions alongside their partners. This shift can create tension, particularly if the husband still subscribes to traditional gender roles.

Money management is another common source of contention. In many African cultures, men are presumed to be the predominant providers. But because of how the economy works, in practice both partners often have to help out financially. People can have very different views on how to earn, spend, or save money, especially with a whole family to consider.

Long-term family members can contribute significantly to conflict on their own. When Africans marry, they are not marrying just two persons; they are marrying two families. This can give in-laws and extended family the impression that they have a say in every aspect of the marriage, from children to finances. For instance, there might be some situations where a couple must choose between being loyal to their partner and honoring their family elders.

Another sensitive issue that can put a strain on African marriages is lack of children or infertility. In many African cultures, the essence of marriage is to propagate. The inability of a couple to have children they are getting is too much pressure, fault, and even a threat to the security of their marriage.

Finally, different religious or spiritual beliefs can pose a major conflict in the relationship—especially in places where interfaith marriages are common. There could be differences in beliefs about religious practices, raising kids spiritually, or participating in traditional rituals.

Stacked logic approach

AND, WHEN THERE ARE disagreements, try to resolve the issues so that it brings understanding and closure instead of pouring gas on the fire. One technique to do it is the "I" sentence. Avoid accusing someone, as it may cause them to become defensive. Instead, try using "I" statements to explain how you feel and what you need. You might say something like, "I feel powerless and unappreciated when I have to take on all the household duties by myself," rather than, "You never pitch in with the household work."

Another useful skill is active listening. That means really listening to your partner and attempting to understand their perspective without interrupting or creating arguments in your head. Rephrase what you heard to ensure you interpreted it correctly. That shows respect and usually helps defuse a tense situation.

Also, remember to stay focused on the issue at hand and avoid bringing up old grievances or making personal attacks on your partner. Avoid making sweeping statements or generalizations that may cause your partner to feel unfairly judged by you. Instead, zero in on the solution to the problem.

A third key component of a constructive case is timing. It should be done when both individuals are calm and mentally and emotionally equipped to hold a good discussion. When one or both are tired, stressed, or emotionally activated, attempts to correct a problem will likely make the situation worse, not better.

Strategies for compromise and negotiation

THEIR JUDGMENTS ALWAYS point to their means of justifying marriage, and compromises become the key to resolving disagreements. Both people need to be willing to accommodate the other to come up with a way to engage that suits both their needs and values. It helps to start with common ground. Even when people are extremely angry at one another, they almost always share some goals or values that could help them find a way to come to a solution.

The "win-win" approach is particularly effective when negotiating a marriage. It is not necessary to view disagreements as contests where only one party can emerge victorious. Instead, they ought to try to find a solution that satisfies them both. This could entail coming up with innovative solutions to problems and exploring unconventional approaches to optimize options that neither partner had previously explored.

It also helps to know which problems are priorities and be prepared to concede on lesser issues. Arguments don't always have to be fatal. By strategically choosing your battles and reaching compromises on smaller issues, you can cultivate goodwill that can be utilized to resolve larger issues in the future.

Here's another excellent approach: the "trial period" approach. If you're having trouble finding a long-term solution, it may be reasonable to work out a temporary agreement, with the understanding that you'll both review it after a designated period of time. This can help resolve a stalemate and also give both sides a chance to see if a proposed solution works without feeling like they are making a lifelong commitment.

Cultural approaches to conflict resolution. Bear in mind that there are many ways to solve disagreements in African countries that can be applied to the problems in marriage. In most African societies, people emphasize the importance of the entire group working together to solve issues. That's why involving recognized elders or community leaders as mediators can help almost all couples find a solution that would be suitable for both of them.

Even though it contradicts the Western idea of marital privacy, African couples benefit from the guidance of external forces. The concept of "Ubuntu," which means unity and how people are connected, can be a strong aspect that can help African couples resolve their differences. From this concept emerges the obligation of people to think of how their actions are affecting not only their partners but their families and communities.

It might be easier for couples to get over their issues and find answers that are beneficial for the whole family if they stop thinking of the disagreements only from their point of view. Additionally, forgiveness and peacemaking are also essential in many African societies. People in some countries believe that being able to forgive and move on means being strong and wise rather than weak.

This belief can help couples get back to normal after a fight and regain trust and harmony in their relationships. For instance, traditions and rituals can be helpful for easy cohabitation. In case of a severe argument, a couple may engage in a ritualistic cleanse or makeup in certain African cultures. In turn, such rites can provide them with what is essentially a fresh start, inspiring them to be more serious about their marriage.

Given the above information, it becomes clear that the ability to speak and solve disputes is essential to keeping peace in African marriages.CSS can change controversial issues into opportunities for both sides to grow and connect by learning about the topics that lead individuals to argue. Of course, how to argue constructively, how to locate common ground, and customs. The subsequent theme, parenting with intention, will be addressed in the next chapter.

Here is a preview of how couples can collaborate to elevate young people who are familiar with their cultural traditions and better prepared for life in the 21st century. While most would prefer to emphasize the children's upbringing and the challenges with maintaining modern norms, African American parents can teach their own children how to cope with a harsh reality.

Chapter 4: Parenting with Purpose

Moving beyond discussing how to solve issues in marriage, we will now talk about parenting, which is another crucial aspect for maintaining peace in the family. In Africa, a child is not simply an independent person under the care of an adult, and the act of nurturing isn't a mere chore but a sacred responsibility that is instrumental in the future of our mind, community, and country. This chapter discusses the delicate balance between traditional parenting advice and new-age methods. It gives you inspiration for raising your kids with meaning and purpose.

Striking a balance between modern and old-fashioned parenting

IN AFRICA, A PARENT is good based on cultural practices passed down through generations. In these traditional ways, people learn to respect their leaders, act responsibly in the interest of the community, and understand the value of virtue. But grandparents feel caught because the world is changing so fast these days that they can't help but want to break out of the things that worked for their parents.

Unlike in traditional African parenting, when parents are more authoritative and used to children following their rules unquestioningly. This parenting style emphasizes rules, respect, and children's place within their family and community. There is a Yoruba saying that says, "A child that we refuse to build will sell the house that we built after all. This does not sound like the way this idea goes: children need boundaries in order to be good, responsible people as adults.

Modern parenting, however, tends to be more influenced by Western ideals and is more child-centric and indulgent. These approaches emphasize open dialogue, nurturing feelings, and promoting independence. Parents are often advised to view their children as distinct individuals with their own thoughts and feelings who have a right to respect and autonomy.

Strive to get these two methods of upbringing working together well. The balanced manner enables parents to cling to traditional values while also keeping up with the times. An example would be that although traditional methods such as teaching respect and discipline can be used, families can also apply new ways of communicating, like being open and providing positive feedback.

Striking this balance is how some parents are adopting a style called "authoritative parenting." Traditional African parenting is about establishing boundaries and high expectations. This, by contrast, emphasizes warmth, communication, and reasoning, the hallmarks of more modern styles. Authoritative parents tell their children why they have certain rules, and they listen to what their children have to say—but kids don't necessarily get to do what they want at the end.

Consider Mrs. Adebayo, a Nigerian mother of three who struggled to find this balance. She grew up in a strict household and initially did that with her children. She did notice, however, that her eldest child became rebellious and withdrawn. After attending a workshop about parenting, Mrs. Adebayo started to talk more openly and spare a mental thought for her children. She adhered to her rules of respect and good behavior, but she explained her thought process to her kids and listened to their responses. Over time, her relationships with her kids and the behavior of the family overall improved tremendously.

How to Discipline Your Child Now and As They

Grow

CHILD CARE IN AFRICA is a skill honed through cultural practice carried from generation to generation. Traditions such as this help instill respect (for leaders), responsibility (for the community), and the importance of the moral compass. However, in the landscape of today, where change comes at a feverish pace, parents often feel trapped, unable to reconcile their old philosophies with new approaches to parenting.

In Africa, when parents bring up their children the traditional way, they expect their children to be obedient and do as they say without question. This style of parenting emphasizes rules, respect, and the child's position in the family and society. Yoruba people have this saying: "The child who we refuse to build grows to sell the house that we build. This statement encapsulates the idea that children need a strict routine to develop into responsible individuals.

In contrast, modern Western styles of parenting tend to be child-centered and more permissive. These approaches emphasize open discussion, caring for feelings, and fostering independence. They encourage parents to think of their children as individual people with their own ideas and emotions who are entitled to be respected and left in peace.

Applying a combination of both of these methods is the secret to good parenting in contemporary African societies. It would help parents to bridge family values with the evolving world in a global setting. Parents in general can continue to focus on traditional values of respect and discipline with new-age approaches like open communication and positive reinforcement.

A method recommended by experts for achieving this balance is "authoritative parenting." This is the best of both modern and traditional African parenting styles. It maintains high standards and clear boundaries but promotes warmth, discussion, and reasoning, which are key components of contemporary approaches. Authoritative parents explain the reasoning behind their rules and are willing to listen to their kids, even if they ultimately don't agree with them.

Take the case of Mrs. Adebayo, a Nigerian mother of three who struggled to find this balance. She grew up in a strict household and initially brought up her children in the same manner. But she noticed that her oldest child grew rebellious and estranged from the rest of the family. After going through parenting training, Mrs. Adebayo began to speak more openly and offer more emotional support in how she raised her children. She maintained her rules around respect and good behavior, but she explained to her children why she held that perspective and listened to what they had to say. Eventually, her relationships with her children and their conduct in general improved significantly.

Tips for encouraging independence and responsibility in kids

IN MOST AFRICAN COUNTRIES, children are viewed as dependent on their parents until late in life. However, early on teaching dependent and responsible attitudes in kids is crucial in order to prepare them for the challenges of today. That doesn't necessarily mean abandoning cultural beliefs about the way families should depend on one another. It means ways to increase independence in the family and society.

Providing children with appropriate chores and tasks is another way to help them be more self-sufficient. Doing so teaches children practical skills, and they also feel they are part of the family. "All my kids have had their own chores since they were 5," said Mr. Owusu, a dad of Ghanaian descent. My youngest watered the plants, my middle child washed the dishes, and my oldest helped me cook. They are proud of what they have accomplished and are learning life skills.

Another key aspect of promoting freedom is the encouragement of individuals making decisions. For little kids, this can begin with small decisions, such as choosing their clothing or deciding between two foods. As they get older, kids can make larger choices that affect their lives, such as choosing extracurricular activities or discussing their goals for the school year.

Freedom and responsibility are inextricably linked. You have to teach kids that they are responsible for what they do. This necessitates empowering them to confront the repercussions of their choices, regardless of the outcome. For instance, if a kid fails to pack their sports equipment for practice, don't rush to deliver it to them. Instead, Shyiak said put the onus on them if they cannot fully be involved. This lets them know the importance of planning ahead and being responsible with their things.

Another critical area of development that conventional parenting typically overlooks is financial independence. If kids learn how to handle money at an early age, they can be successful later on in life. They could also help you with this by giving you a salary and teaching you how to make a budget, save money, and wisely choose to spend your money.

Dr. Nkosi, an education expert from South Africa, argues that it has never been so critical to strike a balance between independence and traditional values. "We want our children to be self-reliant, but not at the expense of our communal traditions." The purpose is to breed people who can sustain themselves and understand their role in the household and society.

Overcoming the unique challenges of African parenting

PARENTING IN AFRICA has its own challenges to navigate. Cultural expectations can be very challenging to cope with in an increasingly modern world. Many parents struggle to raise their children in accordance with traditional values and prepare them for an increasingly interconnected future.

Take the problem of language, for example. In many African countries, kids learn more than 1 language. So they speak a local language at home, the state language in public, and English or French in school. This diversity of languages is a benefit, but it is also a challenge. Parents must decide which languages to prioritize and try to keep their kids in touch with their culture while also learning the languages they'll need to succeed in school and the workplace.

Another job has to do with dealing with touchy issues that might otherwise risk disapproval in normal times. Because things like sex education, mental health, and evolving roles of gender are important topics, even if they are uncomfortable or against traditional standards, open conversations with kids about these topics should occur. A Senegalese mother, Mrs. Diallo: "When my daughter began asking questions about puberty, I felt so uncomfortable at first. In my society, we do not really talk about these things. But I also knew that if I didn't give her accurate information, she might find it from someone else that wasn't as reliable. So I learned more about her and spoke to her in an honest but age-appropriate way.

Technology and social media effects are another thing that makes it difficult for African parents. Kids require the ability to utilize technology to be able to thrive in the future, but in most cases, parents feel that the internet and social media could harm their kids' morals and behavior. Striking the right balance between allowing kids to use technology for good and protecting them from its bad applications requires ongoing education and healthy dialogue.

The urbanization trend is also bringing its own challenges, along with alternative family arrangements. As more families move into cities and become nuclear families, the normal ways extended families help one another have been, in many ways, upended. That it might leave parents feeling isolated and stressed. New support networks need to be created, and ways to keep the extended family in touch need to be found for urban parents.

African parenting is hard enough without us worrying about money problems. Parents in many countries struggle to provide their children with even the necessities of life and help fund their education and future. This can make it difficult to agree on how to share resources and place enormous stress on family ties.

The first step, according to Nigerian family therapist Dr. Okafor, is to be flexible. "The goal is to retain our core values but be willing to change the way we do things. We have to instruct our kids about the world they'll live in, not the world we lived in, and to do that, we need to keep learning and adapting.

Last but not least, from a purposeful parenting perspective within an African context, parenthood is a hard and important job. By balancing custom and modernity, using age-appropriate and positive discipline, developing independence and responsibility, and tackling the problems of our time, we can raise kids who are proud of their culture but ready to take on the world.

In the other chapter, we will discuss another crucial ingredient for family harmony: finding the right balance between work and family. On a continent whose work demands are increasing and whose family dynamics are shifting, this balance is more important than ever to address. We will explore strategies for time management, achieving a work-life balance in African societies, involving your family in household chores, and navigating the often conflicting demands of work and family life.

Chapter 5: Juggling Work and Family

After the turmoil of parenting, we now focus on a new fundamental aspect of family life: balancing work and family responsibilities. In many African societies, the competing demands of career and family often lead to stress and tension at home. In this chapter, we will discuss some approaches that can help you find your way in this minefield and strike a balance between your work life and your home life.

Time management is at the heart of successfully balancing work and family commitments. In the shadows of our busy world, it sometimes seems like there are never enough hours in the day to cross items from our to-do lists. It can be a challenge to balance your career with raising a family, but with strategic planning and proper time priority, finding a way to attend to both of them adequately is possible.

An effective way to manage your time is to plan your schedule properly, which factors in all your daily activities such as work time, family time, and self-care. Seeing your day this way will help you spot chunks of time that are being wasted and reassign them to more productive purposes. For example, you realize you are spending an hour every night scrolling through social media when you could be using those same minutes helping your children with their homework or engaging in meaningful conversation with your spouse.

It's also important to learn the craft of prioritization. Not all tasks are equal, and learning the difference between urgent and important is critical. In the book "The 7 Habits of Highly Effective People," Stephen Covey coined the idea of the Eisenhower Matrix, where tasks are scattered in 4 quadrants according to how urgent and important they are. When you put your attention and energy toward important but not urgent tasks, you avoid the anxiety of putting out fires and instead work toward your long-term goals, at work and at home.

Saying no is another important skill associated with time management. Many cultures in Africa strongly value community and social obligations that can sometimes conflict with family responsibilities. So yes, you should maintain social connections, but you also should set boundaries and know when you need to prioritize the needs of your nuclear family. That can mean declining invitations to social events or curbing your involvement in community activities during especially busy seasons at work or when your family needs more of you.

African culture doesn't make it as clear as western culture that people have two parts of their lives: work life and life at home. This can make it hard to find a good work-life balance. Most African nations have a more blurred line between work and home lives, with aunties, uncles, and neighbors all exerting some influence over personal decisions. This can make it challenging to distinguish between work and personal time.

The key here is communication, both with your employer and with your family, about what you need and expect from each of them. Some African jobs care more about work-life balance and have policies to ensure that employees successfully juggle both work and personal responsibilities. Be open with your supervisor about options to work modified hours or from home and discuss the possibility of these arrangements if you're in that position.

At the same time, it's important to temper expectations with your family regarding your work obligations. This could mean explaining to kids that you can't always be there for every school function or working with your spouse to determine how to divide household duties in a way that balances your two work schedules. Good communication will help you at work and at home.

A critical strategy for managing work-family balance is to involve family members in household responsibilities. Even if they work full-time jobs, in many African households, the woman still carries the bulk of domestic responsibilities. This lopsided approach to work can result in burnout and resentment, which can fracture family harmony. To that end, a more equitable approach to household management needs to be nurtured.

You can start by holding family meetings where household chores and responsibilities are discussed and assigned. Assign age-appropriate chores to children, teaching them valuable life skills and lightening the overall load. For couples, making a joint calendar or work list can help ensure that work is distributed fairly and that each half of the partnership knows what needs to be done. Keep in mind that you are not aiming for perfect equality around spending time on specific tasks, but rather something that feels fair and manageable for everyone.

Also, in the spirit of household management, think about how technology can help you become more efficient. There is no shortage of apps and digital tools that can help with meal planning, grocery shopping, and coordinating family schedules. Although systems that rely heavily on technology can prove to be both impractical and inconvenient, there are systems that use technology well, making life easier and allowing one to have more time and energy to spend with family.

Perhaps the hardest part of balancing work and family in African societies is dealing with the demands of one with the expectations of family. That said, pressure to do well in their career has affected a large portion of professionals, considering some of them want to provide their family with the best or to just fulfill the potential of what society has labeled as a successful life. On the flip side, there are strong social norms around family obligations, especially with regard to caring for aging parents or joining extended family gatherings.

At the same time, to help you traverse these conflicting demands, it is vital to cultivate a strong sense of self-awareness of your own priorities and values. Use it to think about what really matters to you and the immediate family. As much as we all need to honor the cultural traditions and family duties that come with our background, we must also find the balance between what is an obligation and that of being a source of work-life imbalance? Be firm but polite about your limits, explaining your own constraints and suggesting alternative means of fulfilling your family role when you can.

It's also essential to create a support system to help you with both work and family responsibilities. This support system could include trusted colleagues who can step in for you if necessary, family members who can assist with child or eldercare, or friends who can provide emotional support when you're under pressure. I am sure you have heard this before; do not shy away from asking for help if you need it. African culture of unity and ubuntu reminds you that your well-being is interconnected with others, thus you need to rely on people to support you.

We are constantly evolving and navigating this work-life-family dynamic. What works for your family at one point in life may have to be adjusted as the situation continues to evolve. Expect to re-evaluate your plans frequently; communicate with your family and your employer about what is working and what needs to change.

The role of extended family is next on the list of family dynamics in African societies. Then we'll explore how to pass through these challenging dynamics while preserving the harmony and equilibrium of your nuclear family unit. Recognizing the individuality of being part of an extended family and multiple generations at that can help you develop a rounded family unit that meets the needs of your nuclear family while remaining true to tradition.

Chapter 6: Embracing Extended Family Dynamics

The rounded nuclear reactor is the most dominant form of the African family. They consist of a web of rich and complex relationships that have underpinned societies across the continent for centuries. Now, having discussed the challenges of juggling work versus family time, we'll turn to another topic of import: extended family ties. These constitute a huge part of African society and play a huge role in family harmony.

The importance of extended family in African culture

IN AFRICAN CULTURES, grandparents, aunts, uncles, cousins, grandparents, and some who are not related by blood but have been family for years are family. This expansive sense of family has roots in African practices and serves various purposes, including keeping cultural history alive and providing social support.

In Africa, the axis of the extended family structure has historically operated as a social safety net, with relatives helping one another in both good times and bad, pooling resources, and raising kids together. It is typical for grandparents to have a prominent role in raising a child, for cousins to be raised together, or for aunts and uncles to fund their nieces' and nephews' college education. This connection to people provides a security and sense of belonging that is very central to Africanness.

The extended family framework also retains cultural information and customs. Elders are revered for their wisdom and experience; they frequently help to resolve disputes among family members and preserve historical practices. These cultural values are transmitted across generations through narratives, traditions, and collective decision-making in this extended family.

However, as African cultures become increasingly modern and urban, the traditional structure of extended families is encountering fresh challenges. Work or school migration, meanwhile, can strain family bonds. Conversely, economic pressures and evolving social norms could result in family units growing smaller. Despite these problems, extended family remains highly valued in African society. This necessitates finding a balance between preserving the past traditions and adapting to contemporary life.

Boundaries with in-laws and relatives

THE EXTENDED FAMILY system has a lot of merits but can also go south into stress and disagreement if there are no clear rules that are being followed. Setting boundaries with in-laws and other siblings is a vital skill for maintaining peace with the family of origin but also protecting the unity of the married family; it promotes resilience and stops familial disruptive behavior from re-entering the married family.

One of the major challenges married people are faced with in countries in Africa is the expectation from their in-laws that they should have input into their daily lives at all times. This can range from offering unwanted advice about how to raise a child to demanding handouts to showing up frequently and without a cue. To remedy this, partners need to first establish that they are united by discussing what limits work for their family and clearly, but politely, communicating those limits to their extended family.

This is why you need to be kind to your culture when you set up limits. Many Africans, particularly those who work with older people, find it rude to argue or refuse outright. Instead, couples can take subtler approaches, like gradually reducing the number of visits or redirecting the subject of talk away from inflaming issues. You want to be firm and strong but also respectful of the role of the extended family.

In many cases, especially, it's really difficult to evade financial limits. In most African households, wealth is collectivist, so those who have more than their less fortunate relatives are expected to support them. This is a nice way of helping each other out, but one might find it hard to cope if one is careless. Couples are urged to have candid discussions about their money and agree on how much family support they can offer. As one example, they might earmark a portion of monthly income to support extended family members or provide non-financial support (e.g., job leads, skill development).

Another key aspect of setting boundaries is protecting the couple's right to decide for themselves. Make big life decisions—about job moves, child rearing, and where to live. It's nice to get some guidance from family members who have gone that route before, but ultimately the couple should decide. This can be stated respectably but firmly so that it avoids the anger and preserves the couple's sense of freedom within the family system.

Building good relations with in-laws

WHILE THIS CAN PRESENT problems, if you want your family to communicate well, it's important to maintain solid relations with distantly related families. Such ties can provide all kinds of mental support, practical help, and cultural exposure that benefit the entire family—especially the children.

Scheduling family events or rituals that gather extended family members together is a good way to reinforce healthy connections. These can be Sunday dinners occurring weekly, family parties occurring once per year, cultural celebrations, etc. These types of events help people negotiate their relationships, create stories with one another, and work through issues in a lighthearted environment.

Furthermore, it is important to reach out to significant-distance relatives personally. For instance, they might call their grandparents regularly, spend time with their cousins, or ask respected aunts and uncles for assistance. Maintaining these connections helps you create a support network that can be extremely useful when needed.

Asking extended family members to be involved in major decisions and activities in your life can also strengthen the legacy of positive relationships. This does not mean giving up power; it means being respectful of their role in your life. For instance, seeking the approval of an elder before devoting one's life to a radical change or having the grandparents name the child can do wonders to strengthen familial ties.

In the digital age, keeping in touch with family members who live far away—especially when time zones are a factor—has become much easier through technology. Video calls, WhatsApp groups for families, and sharing picture albums are all helpful ways to keep in touch and engage in each other's lives.

What they are is that you treat these partnerships with a sense of greed and desire that you have a lot to give and a lot to receive. It's natural to wonder about how your extended family can contribute to your well-being, but ask yourself what you can do to improve theirs, too. It might mean helping them when it's necessary, sharing your skills or resources, or just being there for them at a time when they really need comfort.

Facing family involvement and expectations

DEALING WITH MEDDLING and expectation management might be one of the trickiest aspects of handling an extended family dynamic. In many African cultures, it can be difficult to distinguish between helpful involvement and intrusive influence. This can lead to family stress and discord.

Family interference may take many forms, from offering unwanted advice about personal issues to attempting to influence major life decisions. It's almost always rooted in genuine care and concern, but no less difficult to navigate. One solution is to see that the person who is intervening is very, very committed to being helpful and, at the same time, politely asserting your own independence. You might start with, "Thank you for caring about our kids' education. We appreciate your experience and thought of such when we made our decision."

Expectations from others can also create stress, particularly when they do not align with the couple's own needs or desires. These might have to do with a person's career, the number of children they have, or practices relating to or adherence to old customs. This is something that should be discussed candidly between the couple and with the rest of the family. Justify your perspective and decisions, demonstrating that you considered theirs, even if you chose a different path.

In some cases, family demands or meddling may be too much or harmful. With these people, you may need to impose stricter limits—or limits—even stop communicating with them for some time. As a last resort, counsel should only be given cautiously and, if possible, with support from a family elder or someone who is familiar with the cultural background.

It's also worth noting that family demands and meddling tend to escalate during major life transitions like getting married, having a child, or switching careers. Preparing for such occasions and planning how to deal with increased family involvement can be helpful in preventing arguments from escalating.

Cultural norms around helping struggling family members or caring for aging parents can create issues, too, particularly when they clash with a couple's own financial or lifestyle goals. Answering these demands requires you to communicate, consider alternative solutions to problems, and sometimes be willing to seek remedies that serve as a compromise between parental authority and personal space.

Having established how extended families operate, the truth is that these relationships can be complex and at times challenging, but they also provide a unique depth and variety that are incredibly significant. One must reconcile cultural practices with family traditions, as well as the functional demands and limitations of the nuclear family. In the next chapter, we will discuss another large topic related to family harmony: how to be wise about money so that family members can flourish. We've discussed communication, setting limits, and mutual respect as approaches to handling relationships with extended family. The same ideas will help us tackle the sensitive topic of family funds.

Chapter 7: Financial Wisdom for Family Prosperity

Having just written about the complexities of having a large family, let's talk about one of the most important aspects of family life that plays at the core of so many challenges and opportunities that we face: how we manage our money. In many African homes, this money etiquette is often tied to cultural values, ancestral responsibilities, and aspiration for progress from one generation to the next. This chapter will describe how families can navigate these extraordinary circumstances and lay a strong financial foundation for the future.

The Art of Budgeting for African Families

AFRICAN FAMILIES MUST excel in budgeting, as their income must cover both personal and extended family needs. A comprehensive spending plan should start with a detailed understanding of all your income sources and expenses. Because solidarity is emphasized in many African countries, this makes it difficult to apply conventional budgeting practices.

It also provides a good method, which has been modified for use in Africa, known as the "envelope system." And one way to do this is to put the money in separate bags or (in more modern cases) mobile money accounts for each type of cost. You might set aside one package for daily living expenses, one for school fees, and one for aiding extended family members, for example. Separating the funds in this way can allow families to visually see just how much they are spending and ensure that they satisfy their core needs before employing any further expenditure.

You also want to consider illegal income streams. These are typical in many African nations that have seasonal and informal work. With a flexible planning process that adjusts for a range of incomes, families can remain financially sustainable year after year. That could entail preparing a "lean budget" for times in the year when dollars are tighter and a "comfort budget" for months when money is flush.

Community fundraisers, or "haram bee," are another key consideration when planning in African homes. Many families participate in or plan these events to fundraise and cover the costs of big events like weddings, funerals, or school bills. They can let this guide them so as to avoid things becoming too costly, as they include expected haram bee payments in the family budget.

You can never overestimate how important women are in handling family finances. In most African societies, keeping the household running and settling the bills was traditionally the responsibility of the woman. Teaching women about money matters and involving them in every aspect of family expenditure can prove to be an effective way of budgeting and allocating resources.

"As you teach a woman about money, you teach a whole family," one Kenyan finance expert said. Women are often able to see the needs of the entire family and can be excellent managers of household resources when they are equipped and empowered to do so.

How to Teach Children Basic Money Management Skills

IN AFRICA, FINANCIAL literacy is an important life skill that is poorly addressed in formal education. For that reason, it is up to parents to make sure their children cultivate a beneficial relationship with money early on. This kind of education is not just about teaching your child to save but also about teaching them the value of financial responsibility, entrepreneurship, and philanthropy.

The best business practice is to jumpstart children early around appropriate family/financial talks. This may involve teaching basic concepts, such as saving and spending, to younger children and gradually introducing more complicated topics like investing and budgeting as children grow older. This exercise is successful for many African family families using traditional savings methods as tools for teaching. The idea of "susu" in West Africa, where small amounts are saved over several days, can be a great method to educate your kids about the magic of saving consistently.

Many cultures in Africa place a high premium on entrepreneurship, so helping your children set up small businesses is an excellent way to teach them how to manage their finances. It could be as basic as helping an owner set up a little vegetable stand where you can help or asking them to wash cars and giving it to the neighbors. In that way, kids learn about profit, loss, customer service, and the importance of hard work.

Teaching children about the cultural aspects of money in African societies is also important. That includes helping them understand things such as communal saving schemes, the obligation to support extended family members, and the need to contribute to causes in the community. Learning to navigate these cultural expectations will help children balance personal financial goals and societal pressures.

In Africa, digital platforms are financial tools for children. In countries like Kenya and Nigeria, mobile money apps aimed at children and parents who are saving are growing in popularity. These tools allow children to learn about contemporary finances still being managed under parental control.

A Ghanaian banker who is a mother of three shared this: "I started giving my kids a small allowance—starting when they were eight years old—with a caveat. They had to split it up into three parts: one for saving, one for spending, and one for donating to a cause of their choosing. This straightforward practice has offered them powerful lessons on financial planning and social stewardship."

For Family Goals: Saving and Investing

WE ARE THERE, AND BACK to drag to a prerequisite of ubuntu, which literally means as the bedrock of many African cultures, the ubuntu is shared, and the shared is unity, where the whole is greater than the individual. In family investments, this communal approach to finances may also pose challenges and opportunities to save and invest for family goals.

The first step in saving effectively is to clarify family financial goals. This could be for short-term goals such as funding a family holiday or longer-term aims like paying for children's schooling or developing a family home. In many African contexts, these ambitions often reach a little further, to encompass extended family members or community projects.

Traditional rotating savings groups—called by different names in different parts of the continent, including "chama" in East Africa and "tontine" in francophone West Africa—can make for effective platforms for disciplined saving. In addition, these groups offer both structure and Africa—can get into the habit of saving regularly while fostering a sense of community and mutual support. But with this, we need to be cautious and can set up really well-managed groups to avoid this issue.

For more formalized savings and investment products, there has been an explosion in accessible financial products in numerous African nations. Mobile money platforms have transformed saving practices so that even people in remote areas can save small amounts of money on a regular basis. Several of these platforms have now started offering goal-based saving features, something that helps families put away savings for particular targets.

Education is often considered one of the most crucial long-term investments for African families. This can mean creating education savings accounts or investing in real estate that is located near good schools so that it can either be utilized as housing for the children (or rented out to fund expenses related to the education itself).

Many African countries consider real estate a solid investment option and view it as a physical asset that does not depreciate. But families need flexibility in their investments. This includes exploring mutual funds, government bonds, or even stocking the stock market if possible and available.

More resourceful families could invest in diaspora bonds^8 or in promising local businesses^9 to build wealth and contribute to national or community development. Countries such as Nigeria and Kenya have already created investment products to specifically reach these diaspora populations and allow them to invest in the development of their homeland.

A financial adviser in Nigeria added that it is best to start young, saying that "most African families wait until they have 'enough' money to start investing. But the important part is to start with what you have, even if it's a little bit a month. Its regular long-term investing that has a way of building true wealth over the long term."

Tackling Financial Issues Specific to African Households

THOUGH SOUND FINANCIAL management principles apply globally, the unique challenges African families face require tailored solutions. Identifying and overcoming these challenges is essential for achieving sustained financial success.

One of the biggest problems is the expectation of financial support for extended families. This "black tax," as it is sometimes known, can place a huge financial strain on a family. Supporting family is an important cultural value, but find balance that does not compromise the financial health of the immediate family.

It is also vital to have clear boundaries and communication around financial assistance. This could mean allocating a certain percentage of income to contribute to the family or collaborating with extended family members to create sustainable solutions, such as funding education or business types rather than ongoing donations.

High spending on key cultural events like weddings and funerals is another issue. These are often of great social significance and can be undertaken at a considerable financial cost. Some families are responding to this by forgoing lavish celebrations or sharing costs with communally saving methods—splitting funds over time.

The other barrier for many African households is informal employment and irregular income streams. This factor of unpredictability may make it difficult to save consistently and plan financially for the long term. Having several sources of income and side businesses makes you more stable overall. Moreover, employing flexible savings approaches that enable variable contributions could help account for income variability.

Formal financial services are still limited in many areas of Africa, especially in rural locations. The good news is that the advent of mobile banking and fintech solutions is helping to close that gap. These technologies expose families to new forms of savings accounts, microloans, and even investment products that may have been considered unreachable.

We cannot ignore the influence of economic uncertainty and elevated inflation rates in some African countries either. In those environments, wealth preservation becomes as important as wealth creation. They may involve investing in inflation-hedging assets, such as real estate, or foreign currency accounts when permitted by law.

One financial planner working in Zimbabwe explained her take: "In hyperinflationary environments, the common advice to 'put away some money' could mean losing value over time." In our clients, we encourage a mindset of value preservation and growth, which may involve investing in livestock, land, or safe foreign currencies—rather than holding cash savings."

In many African countries, there are no comprehensive social security systems available, which means families must plan carefully around retirement and the unexpected, such as health emergencies. Establishing emergency funds and pursuing private pension schemes if available are important steps toward overcoming this challenge.

Gender Digitization Financial Inclusion:

IN ADDITION, THERE is still a challenge that is ongoing in many of these African societies on the disparity between males & females in the area of financial literacy & access to financial services. Women Influence 70% of household purchases, but less than 1 in 3 women are consulted in family financial decisions.

In conclusion, through this journey of financial wisdom for the prosperity of the family, it's apparent that as much as African families have challenges, they also have strengths. For families, that translates to a deep sense of family, creative means of saving together, and greater access to tech-based products to bolster financial success.

In the next article, we are going to talk about another key ingredient to family harmony: clearing marital hurdles. If financial difficulties can challenge a family's resilience, marital issues can also disrupt the foundation of a family's existence. And in the next chapter, we will discuss how to combat things like infidelity and differences in culture or in-laws, which you can go back through into the next chapter hand in hand stronger than ever.

Chapter 8: Overcoming Common Marital Hurdles

Having covered the whole range of topics and issues that contribute to a harmonious house, we dive into some of the more difficult hurdles that couples encounter in their marriage. These barriers, although significant, are not impossible to overcome. However, couples can overcome these challenges and emerge even stronger with the right mindset, compassion, and effort.

Covering infidelity and trust issues

CHEATING ON YOUR SPOUSE can lead to the dissolution of any marriage, particularly in African cultures where family honor and reputation hold significant importance. The act of a partner leaving the relationship is more than just tampering with the fabric of another relationship; infidelity is a betrayal of trust, fundamental to the foundation of the relationship, functioning as it does for the individual unit of two people.

When dealing with an instance of infidelity, the first step in the process is to recognize and affirm the pain and sadness both partners are feeling. The betrayed partner will experience a maelstrom of depression, bewilderment, and self-doubt. It's important to create space for these emotions to be expressed and processed. It may be difficult, but open and honest communication is key during this time.

For the partner who was unfaithful, it is critical that they take full responsibility for what they've done. This necessitates not only a commitment to change their habits but also the level of contrition necessary to acknowledge your mistakes and take the necessary actions to rebuild trust. Responses that are defensive or look to place blame on others will only serve to erode the relationship further.

Rebuilding Trust after Infidelity takes time and effort. This takes time, dedication, and a lot of effort from both parties. The offending partner has to be open to answering questions candidly and to follow up with reassurance when asked. That might mean sharing passwords, checking in regularly, or being open about where and with whom they go.

For the partner who has been betrayed, the process of forgiveness is very personal and often not linear. Always bear in mind that forgiving is not forgetting or accepting the cheating. Instead, it's a choice to continue and to sink more into the relationship.

As both partners learn to live with infidelity, many couples turn to marriage counseling for help. An experienced therapist will offer both partners a safe environment to talk about their feelings, explore their relationship challenges, and come up with a plan for working to rebuild trust and intimacy.

Note, too, that depending on the African culture, traditional conflict resolution practices may be used. This might include some family elders or community leaders trying to broker talks between the couple. As helpful as these approaches can be, it is equally important that they do not belittle the betrayed partner's feelings or rush them to forgive before they are ready to do so.

For the couple, the road to reconciliation will involve grappling with the infidelity, but it should not be limited to just that. That could mean looking at communication breakdowns, unmet needs, or personal insecurities. Addressing the underlying factors will help couples not just move past the infidelity but fortify their bond for future temptations.

You might also like: Infidelity recovery: 5 signs your partner is serious about making it work Remember, recovery from infidelity is possible! Just know that it does require a mutual commitment to the relationship and a desire to do the hard work of rebuilding trust. As African relationship expert Dr. Funke Baffour once said, "Infidelity doesn't have to be the end of a marriage. With work, both individually and as a couple, and with the help of a professional, many couples find that they are able to emerge from this crisis with a more honest, more resilient relationship than before."

Dealing with in-law conflicts

IN MANY AFRICAN CULTURES, marriage is a union between not just two but two families. While this situation can make for a beautiful, colorful tapestry of support and connectivity, there is a potential for enormous, conflicting tension—especially with in-laws.

One of the most common sources of in-law conflict is a tussle for influence over the newlyweds. This is particularly characteristic of traditional environments where parents, especially mothers-in-law, often feel entitled to a considerable voice in the couple's dealings. From financial decisions to child-rearing practices, the scope for disagreement and subsequent resentment is considerable.

The married couple must maintain unity to navigate through these turbulent times. That does not necessarily mean totally breaking away from extended family, but rather creating necessary boundaries to protect the sanctity of the marital relationship. According to Bukky Yusuf, a Nigerian family counselor, a couple must prioritize their relationship above all else. They must collaborate to make decisions and stand by each other to uphold them, even in the face of family pressure.

Dealing with in-law circumstances requires transparency. That includes not just the way the couple talks to each other about in-law considerations, but how they communicate with their families as well. Though mutual respect and cultural awareness are necessary for these discussions, it is especially important to acknowledge the significance of extend in African culture and determine when it is time to end a relationship that involves a husband and wife attempting to establish their osmosis of privacy.

Consider a situation where a mother-in-law frequently visits without prior notice and imparts unwanted advice. The spouse whose parent it is needs to take the lead in working on that kind of wanted behavior, however. They might say something like, "Mom, we love you coming to visit, but we'd really like you to call ahead when you come over. "We're trying to create our own routines as a couple, and while I appreciate your advice, we need to figure this out ourselves."

It's equally important for each partner to negotiate their own family's expectations and behavior. This helps avoid putting the other spouse in the middle or making them the target of resentment. If and when conflicts arise, they are best handled directly in private rather than ignoring tensions that simmer or damaging relationships by airing grievances for everyone to hear during family gatherings.

In other instances, cultural dictates surrounding filial piety may make it hard for someone to stand up to their parents or in-laws. In these moments, it helps to reframe boundary-setting not as a rejection of family but as a way to prioritize building a strong marriage that will serve the whole extended family well in the long run.

Another frequent point of friction with in-laws is financial expectations in African marriages. Expectations of financial support from the married couple by extended family can also lead to strain on the couple and resentment when their resources go to relatives instead of to children and savings. Here, the couple needs to talk about, and reach agreement on, their financial priorities and limits, and then communicate those clearly to their families.

Though working through in-law disputes can be difficult, it should be remembered that you have the potential to also gain lots of support and happiness through these relationships if things can be worked through successfully. Couples can create harmonious relationships that enrich their lives and those of their children by establishing clear boundaries, communicating effectively, and valuing their marriages and their extended families.

Managing differences in religious or cultural beliefs

AFRICAN SOCIETIES ARE as diverse as you can find; hence, marriages are most likely to involve individuals of different religious or cultural backgrounds. These unions can be a rich source of cultural merging and symbiotic education between human beings, but they can also be a very heavy burden if we see that we have fundamental divergences.

Another extreme is the raising of children, where most of the tension between religions and cultures lies. Questions about which faith traditions to follow, which cultural practices to observe, and how to instill values can become ongoing sources of contention if they are not handled thoughtfully.

The solution to these differences is open and honest communication. Couples need to speak candidly about their beliefs, values, and expectations early in a relationship. This does not mean that either partner must compromise their beliefs for the other, but both must be willing to explore their differences with mutual respect, curiosity, and a desire to find common ground.

Dr. Akua Gyamfi, a Ghanaian psychologist, says: "Middle respect is key “in interfaith or intercultural marriages, and the key is not to try to change your partner but to understand and respect their beliefs and practices. Look for ways that your differences can be strengths instead of barriers.”

One strategy that many successful interfaith couples employ is to emphasize the common values that underlie their differing belief systems. For example, both Christianity and Islam emphasize charity, compassion, and moral living. Couples can then use their commonalities as a springboard to create an ethical framework for a life lived together as a family.

Many couples (including some I've personally known to be open to raising their own children in this way) take a mixed approach to raising kids, exposing them to both sets of religious or cultural traditions so they are free to make their own choices when they are old enough to understand. To succeed, both partners need to consciously present their beliefs and practices in a positive manner and not disparage or dismiss the other person's tradition.

A Christian-Muslim couple, for example, might have Christmas and Eid celebrations, teach their children about Jesus as well as Muhammad, and encourage their children to ask questions and explore both faiths. This serves to honor the heritage of both parents and armed children with an immensely applicable cultural and spiritual lens in an increasingly diverse globalized context.

It's also necessary for couples to talk about and make decisions together about how they will navigate potential areas of conflict, such as dietary restrictions, religious holidays, or activities with extended family who may not approve of the interfaith marriage. A plan can keep these challenges from turning into flashpoint sources of conflict.

In some instances, couples might have to create new traditions that incorporate aspects of each of their backgrounds. This can be a wonderful way to honor both heritages while creating something unique for this family. For example, a couple from different ethnic backgrounds could merge the traditions of both cultures in a wedding ceremony or develop family traditions from both cultures.

When disagreements turn into disputes because beliefs are in conflict, it is critical for couples to use empathy and compromise in their conflicts. This could involve rotating where the family goes to various religious or seeking out secular substitutes for practices whose spiritual counterpart brings about discomfort for one partner.

It should be noted that in some cases, there can be a radical conversion of one partner over the course of the marriage. This can be extremely difficult, as it changes the essential nature of the relationship and the understanding that the relationship was based on. When this occurs, patience, understanding, and frequently professional counseling can be significant in assisting the couple to traverse through this change.

Although differences in beliefs can lead to friction, they can also form the bedrock of strength and resilience in a marriage. Embracing their differences through mutual respect, transparency, and creativity can help couples galvanize a family culture that nurtures both their heritages and sets them up for living harmoniously together for many years.

Handling and overcoming infertility and reproductive challenges

HAVING KIDS IS OFTEN considered a cultural and familial obligation rather than a personal choice. When couples experience infertility or reproductive issues, they can create tremendous stress, shame, and conflict both in the marriage and with the extended family.

Recognizing the impact on couples themselves is also important, as this process can be dark and isolating. Feelings of inadequacy, guilt, anger, and depression are normal and should be discussed openly and with empathy. It's essential for couples to create a safe space where they can express these feelings without judgment or blame.

Dr. Nkechi Asogwa, Nigeria's leading fertility specialist, stresses the need for couples to have each other's backs when experiencing infertility: "Infertility is not a 'woman's problem' or a man's problem'—it is a couple's problem. Its couple's journey, and both of you need to approach it like a team, supporting one another throughout the emotional rollercoaster of the journey."

Stigma and social pressure among the most significant issues in African contexts are the stigma and social pressure that often accompany infertility. Intentioned family members may frequently pressure the couple about new children without knowing the questions are painful. In some instances, there can also be hints of polygamy or pressure to divorce if the marriage doesn't yield children.

Couples should set boundaries with family and friends to manage this outside pressure, she said. This could mean having frank discussions about their challenges and requesting empathy and discretion. Sometimes this means setting barriers to those in the couple's life who are not supportive or respectful of their journey.

Education about infertility and the range of treatment options available is also important for couples. Knowing this may help them take control when seeking reproductive care or help them be more successful advocates for themselves in medical contexts. But you need to go about this gathering of information as a team, with both partners on board and clear on next steps.

The costs associated with fertility treatments can be high, especially in settings where they may not be covered by health insurance. This requires honest communication between couples about their financial limits and priorities. This may mean making tough choices about whether and how much to spend on treatments versus other options, such as adoption.

Adoption is a lovely way to expand family, but it can pose challenges in African settings. You may face cultural resistance to the concept of raising a child that you are not biologically connected to. Couples who decide to adopt, however, must be ready to confront these cultural attitudes and to defend their decision to adopt if they go that route.

During the struggle of dealing with infertility, couples need to work at finding the things they can enjoy together without being defined by their ability to reproduce. Some of that might be reviving romance, sharing common interests, or seeking new ways to bond emotionally and physically. As the Kenyan relationship counselor Dr. Catherine Mbau says, "Don't let the pursuit of parenthood eclipse the love and companionship that connected you in the first place."

Support groups can be very helpful for couples facing infertility. Finding others who share your diagnosis or where this has been within family shared experiences can be a comfort, as well as a way of getting practical advice from those who know the realities of such things. In some situations where these types of groups may not be as accessible, you can add online groups and support networks as a helpful alternative.

And it is equally important to take into account the effect of infertility on mental health. Individuals and Couples with Infertility Common reactions include depression and anxiety. Professional help — whether therapy or counseling — can offer tools for addressing these mental health issues and strengthening the relationship.

Whether by choice or circumstance, the idea of living childless becomes a very real consideration for some couples who haven't gotten the baby they hoped for. This choice in some African contexts is extremely difficult, as parenthood is often regarded as a core life stage. This decision often prompts couples to seek out life fulfillment in other ways and learn how to rehash their life goals.

In the end, overcoming infertility and reproductive problems takes time, strength, and a profound commitment to the marriage. With teamwork on these challenges, good communication, attention to learn the variables of both parties in this situation, seeking support if needed, and nurturing the relationship through the process, couples can navigate this challenging road and come out on the other side stronger, whatever the outcome.

As we wrap up this section on navigating the most common married roadblocks, I would like to remind you that every challenge, no matter how hard, is an opportunity to grow and connect deeper. It doesn't matter if you are dealing with infidelity, in-law conflicts, religious differences, or infertility; if you choose to face these obstacles together, in a spirit of empathy, respect, and mutual investment in your relationship, they can be meaningful and transformative. This will be the topic of our next chapter: nurturing emotional bonds that can serve as an anchor to withstand these and other marital storms.

Chapter 9: Nurturing Emotional Bonds

We now embark on a pursuit that is in many ways the final phase of survival, focusing on growing the heart of the family and the emotional bonds that tie us all together through good and bad. In African societies, where the essence fundamentally embraces its root on community and connection, having the skills to build profound and authentic relationships within the family unit is not just a 'bonus'—it is a requisite.

The attic of a long-term relationship: Building and maintaining intimacy

WHILE INTIMACY IS CRUCIAL for any long-term relationship, it frequently suffers as a result of the daily demands of family life. But when extended family, work, and community obligations take priority in many African households, couples may slowly drift apart without realizing it. Intentionality and consistency are the keys to building and maintaining intimacy.

Having regular, quality time together is one of the best ways to encourage intimacy. This doesn't require grand gestures or fancy dates; instead, it's about creating small moments each day to reconnect. For example, many couples have found success with a "daily check-in" ritual, in which they spend 15-20 minutes each day, where they each share thoughts, feelings, and experiences without distractions. This straightforward practice can do wonders to keep partners emotionally in harmony with one another.

Maintaining a strong emotional bond is just as dependent on physical intimacy. Physical expression of love is also very important to many African couples, especially in cultures where public displays of affection are frowned upon, something they often need but find in private. This doesn't need to be sexual; even something as simple as holding hands, hugging, or massaging provides the physical touch that supports that connection.

We also have to recognize that intimacy needs to change with time. What used to fly in the early days of a relationship may not fly as well decades later. As couples develop together, they need to be open to trying different avenues of connection. That could mean they pick up a new hobby together, rethink their sexual relationship, or figure out new ways to show appreciation for one another.

Affectionate and loving behavior in ways that are culturally appropriate

BEYOND A GENERAL DIFFERENCE in communication styles, there are the particularities of African cultures, where love and affection are often expressed in more subtle and indirect ways than we are accustomed to in the West. This doesn't mean that love is any less deep, but that it comes out in a different way and with different expectations. If one wishes to be intimate with other members of the family, he must understand and follow these cultural imperatives.

One such expression that many African families show love through is acts of service. For example, a wife may demonstrate her love by cooking her husband's favorite food, and a husband may act out of love by taking on additional chores to relieve his wife's burden. Born from the same perfumed blood, these acts may seem banal but convey great emotional weight inside the culture.

While we may not be as expressive as certain cultures, when we do express our love, it carries immense power. Many African languages contain endearing terms and phrases that express love, deeply ingrained in each culture. The gravity behind using "mpenzi wangu" (my love) or "moyo wangu" (my heart) in Swahili admits something deeper than words. Intentional and genuine use of these phrases can really bring emotional connections to new heights.

Also, in many African cultures, love and respect are combined. Even when a spouse speaks with deferential language, acts graciously, or otherwise publicly champions their partner's value, it is often considered an action of deep love. Families can build stronger bonds by intentionally creating a culture of respect and appreciation for one another.

Establishing family traditions and rituals

Family traditions and rituals are an important aspect of building emotional connections and a sense of continuity, identity, and belonging. This can be particularly evident in African cultures where the idea of family goes beyond the immediate family unit, such as giving each other gifts and sharing meals; these experiences can form strong ties and lasting memories.

Some traditions may be related to cultural or religious observances, e.g., coming-of-age ceremonies, harvest festivals, or religious holidays. These events are a way for families to unite, reencounter their common patterns of values, and establish a connection with their ancestors and roots. But it's just as important for families to develop their own traditions that reflect their specific dynamics and interests.

As an example, a family could establish a weekly "storytelling night," where family members swap stories about their own experiences or those from their culture. Not only does this provide entertainment, but it also serves as a way to pass down family history and values to younger generations. While another family might establish a tradition of acknowledging and celebrating personal milestones, big or small, building an environment of support and encouragement.

Rituals can also be key to strengthening family ties. These can be as simple as a regular family dinner at which everyone discusses the best part of their day or as grand as a yearly family reunion that reunites extended family members from near and far. The trick is consistency and meaning—these rituals should be things that family members look forward to and that strengthen their sense of connection to one another.

Traditions and rituals should change with the family, but we should also remember at least three things. What is working for a young family with toddlers may need to evolve as those toddlers become teenagers and young adults.

Nurturing emotional intelligence in your family members

EMOTIONAL INTELLIGENCE—THE capacity to recognize, understand, and manage one's own emotions and to empathize with others—is an essential skill for effective relationship management. In the realm of family dynamics, nurturing emotional intelligence can create closer connections, better communication, and more unity in familial relationships.

The initial step for parents in nurturing emotional intelligence is to model it themselves. Children learn mostly by example, and they will absorb how their parents deal with emotions, conflicts, and relationships. And this means parents will need to do their own emotional work—learning to sense and regulate their own emotions and to verbalize and express them in adaptive ways.

A good strategy to encourage emotional intelligence in children is to assist them in naming and understanding how they feel. Rather than dismissing or diminishing a child's feelings, parents can validate them and assist the child with the process of identifying what they're feeling. Instead of "Don't cry," for example, a parent might say, "I see that you are feeling sad. What do you mean that I'm making you feel that way?"

Another important skill in emotional intelligence is teaching empathy. Parents can help develop this skill by prompting children to think about other people's points of view and feelings. This could mean talking about characters' motivations in stories, role-playing various scenarios, or just having kids use their imaginations to consider the impact of their actions on others.

It is also necessary to foster a family environment in which all emotions are accepted and validated, while understanding that some behaviors associated with those emotions may not be. This means giving family members permission to feel angry, sad, or upset without fear of judgment or punishment, but being clear and keeping boundaries around the appropriate behavior.

With higher emotional intelligence, family members are in a better position to manage the intricacies of relationships, both internal and external to the family. This creates deeper and stronger emotional ties between family members—and a more harmonious family as a whole."

As a final note, cultivating emotional intimacy takes purposefulness and intention. In conclusion, African families can build the foundation for emotionally satisfied relationships by prioritizing intimacy and love languages that are significant within their community, developing traditions and rituals, and cultivating emotional intelligence. Going forward, we will discuss how these robust emotional systems allow families to weather crises as a family unit and emerge stronger on the other side.

Chapter 10: Weathering Family Crises Together

So as we near the end of our exploration of African family life, we must take a couple of moments for the many realities of life with family. In the last chapter, we discussed the critical role played by the development of emotional bonds—a powerful basis to build upon for the final chapter. The strength of these bonds usually determines how well a family can weather a crisis.

Families in Africa, like families everywhere, are not immune to crises. Nonetheless, the sociocultural and economic contexts of African households tend to have a significant hand in determining the content of these crises and the strategies deployed to respond to them. In this chapter, we will discuss the common family crises in African contexts, resilience planning, when to seek professional help, and how adversity strengthens family.

Some common family crises in African contexts

AFRICAN FAMILY CRISES manifest in various forms and sizes, frequently serving as microcosms of the challenges encountered by African societies. Economic insecurity is one of the most widespread crises. In much unemployment, a struggling economy, high unemployment, and sudden job loss can throw a family into financial chaos—and that's even before cost-of-living increases or, in many places, rising taxes hit. This lack of economic certainty can have a negative domino effect, leading to things like food insecurity, a lack of ability to afford education or health care, and ultimately homelessness.

According to Dr. Amina Sow, a family therapist in Senegal, "economic crises are notably complicated for African families due to the extended family system. When one family member loses a job, it tends to have a ripple effect not only on their immediate family but also the larger network of relatives who rely on them for support."

Health crises are also at the forefront of the African family picture. The HIV/AIDS comparison has taken a toll on families on the continent; many children have been orphaned or left abandoned to live with elderly grandparents. More recently, specific outbreaks of diseases like Ebola have actually presented acute crises to families in affected areas. More familiar health problems, like malaria or complications during childbirth, can become full-blown crises in many places, where access to quality care is limited.

Political instability and conflict are another category of crises that can have a major impact on African families. Civil wars, coups, and ethnic conflicts can scatter families in flight and split family members, causing trauma that lasts for years. In more stable countries, too, political tensions can drive families apart, particularly when members come to have opposing political views.

Family life in Africa is also affected by cultural and social crises. This can range from clashes due to different values across generations to a struggle between traditional ways of life and modern, technology-driven lifestyles, or even problems caused by urbanization and changing family traditions. A family crisis may arise, for example, when young adults marry outside their ethnic group or religion against the wishes of their parents and extended family.

"In many African societies, crises that beset families tend not to stop at nuclear family levels," Professor Chidi Anyanwu, a sociologist at the University of Nigeria, explains. Because what would be regarded as a personal issue in Western settings can advance to a crisis that involves the entire extended family and even the community. This can also complicate the resolution of the crisis and offer a larger support network.

Environmental crises, though less commonly mentioned, are increasingly pertinent for African families. Droughts, floods, and other natural disasters caused by climate change can obliterate agricultural livelihoods, force migration, and instill long-term economic hardship in families.

Familiarizing yourself with these common crises is the first step to creating approval strategies to ease them. When discussing topics that are challenging, like war or political turmoil, it is important to note that with all the crises, African families have shown incredible resilience.

Building resilience and coping skills

RESILIENCE—THE CAPACITY to recover from or adjust to misfortune or change—is a critical quality for families facing crises. Resilience in the west relates more to psychological strength, whereas focus in Africa might be more on cultural strengths, community support, and traditional wisdom coupled with modern coping strategies.

One of the important elements about developing resilience is open communication in the family. The crisis is a time for all family members to feel that they can safely share their fears, concerns, and needs. This transparency will help avoid misunderstandings and result in all parties involved feeling desired and heard. "Set regular family meetings when big crises hit," says Dr. Fatima Abdullahi, a family counselor in Nigeria. Such could be formal sit-down discussions or informal chats during meal times. Maintaining open lines of communication is crucial.

One other crucial strategy is to keep routines and rituals as much as possible during a crisis. It can foster a sense of normalcy and stability, especially for children. Family rituals—whether daily prayer times, weekly family dinners, or annual celebrations—can be beacons during tumultuous times.

Part of resilience is also flexibility. This is sometimes expressed in the adaptability of traditional practices to new circumstances among African families. Economic crises have revealed that many families have found innovative ways to unite, such as pooling resources, providing support, and thinking creatively. This could mean adult children moving back in with parents or entire extended families sharing living spaces to save money.

One of the most important means of building resilience is to develop a family way of dealing with problems. This means discussing issues, working on ideas, and enacting plans together. Families can draw on their collective wisdom and build their capacity to meet challenges ahead of them through the involvement of all family members in this process, including children's age-appropriate involvement.

For many African families, spiritual and religious beliefs are key to forging resilience. During difficult times, faith can provide comfort, meaning, and a sense of purpose. Religious communities can provide practical aid as well, from food and shelter to emotional counseling.

Dr. Kwame Osei, a psychologist in Ghana, stresses that it's important to build a positive outlook: "Encourage people in the family to focus on what they can do, not what they cannot do. Guide them in recognizing their strengths and prior successes in overcoming obstacles. This can instill confidence and hope, even amid sizable hurdles."

Your physical and mental health matter even in times of crisis. Promoting regular physical activity, balanced nutrition, and sufficient sleep can inspire physical and emotional fortitude. Mindfulness techniques (adapted to suit African contexts) are another effective stress- and anxiety-management tool.

Building and maintaining social connections is also critical for the development of family resilience. The traditional idea of family in Africa goes beyond the nuclear family structure. Building connections with extended family members, neighbors, and community members can help develop a strong support network to rely on in times of need.

Though family and community support can be invaluable, at times it takes a professional to help families through their crises. Sadly, in many North American contexts, stigma, a dearth of mental health services, and financial insufficiencies render seeking such help difficult or even impossible.

So making efforts to destigmatize mental health support and professional counseling is key. According to Dr. Miriam Nketsiah, a family therapist based in Kenya, there is a common misconception that seeking professional help implies a family's failure or exposing personal issues in public. We must shift from this mentality and realize that asking for help is not a sign of weakness."

However, a culturally competent practitioner would recognize the unique dynamics of African families and the stigma attached to seeking professional help. This could include traditional healers, religious leaders, or Western-trained therapists who acknowledge African cultural contexts.

Community-based organizations and non-governmental organizations can often offer helpful support services, such as counseling, financial advice, and practical assistance. These organizations might be much easier to access than and/or more culturally oriented than formal mental health services in many areas.

Support groups can also be finding sources for families in crisis. These groups can be specifically organized or tailored toward individual problems (such as HIV/AIDS support groups) or broader family predicaments, and they offer a chance to share experiences, learn coping strategies, and make connections with people going through similar ordeals.

Loosening the restrictions on tele therapy, for example, or less formal mental health services offered by community health worker programs, may be less expensive and more popular in situations in which patients face barriers to accessing formal services. Mobile phone-based counseling services have shown that they can reach families in remote areas or those unable to access in-person services because of stigma or logistical difficulties.

It's also useful to understand that various family members may require different forms of support. Children especially might benefit from having professional guidance to help them process and navigate family crises. They may be able to connect you with schools, community centers, or child-focused NGOs.

Building family bonds through adversity

CRISES CAN PULL FAMILIES apart, but they can also bring families together—if done with intention and care. The collective experience of overcoming challenges can foster a profound sense of solidarity and resilience in a family.

The crisis is also a chance to bring the family closer, and to do that, one can tell a story to each other, especially in the home. Encourage family or close people to tell their stories about how they feel and their fears, which helps to build empathy and strengthen relationships.

This can be especially helpful when older generations share stories of old crises and how they got through them, serving as both context and motivation for younger people.

Solving problems collaboratively can also strengthen ties among families. If your family members are working together to tackle challenges, it strengthens their sense of unified purpose and accomplishment. This can manifest as dividing responsibilities, pooling resources, or collaborating to devise innovative solutions to problems.

It can bring positivity to an otherwise tough family face if you are grateful for it until the last moment. Have all family members take turns on those occasions sharing what they admire about each other and the family as a whole.

Establishing new family traditions or rituals in response to crises can also be a powerful bonding experience. For instance, if the family was going through some financial struggles, they might begin a tradition of having "creativity nights," where they brainstorm free or cheap ways to have fun together.

Dr. Aminata Diop, a family researcher in Senegal says, "Crises often make families reprioritize and highlight what is important. Although difficult, this process can create deeper, more real relationships in the family."

It is also important to acknowledge little wins and milestones on the journey. This should include acknowledging and celebrating family milestones and achievements, which can help build morale and make the family feel even more united together.

In the end, weathering crises together, collectively, may even forge a narrative of risk-taking, strength, and perseverance within our families. They can take pride in this narrative, bond over it, and feel a sense of kinship not just in the story but for generations.

In closing, as we unpack family life and the crisis of family life in African contexts, it's clear that although crises may be inevitable, they need not define a family. And through communication, flexibility, suitable external help, and determination to strengthen ties, African families can not only endure crises but also become stronger and more united after them. By doing so, they uphold a long history of family resilience that has characterized African societies for centuries.

Conclusion

In "Harmony at Home," we've set off on a journey to investigate the complexities of African family life and relationships. From core values of familial unity through to the challenges of work-life balance, we've explored the realities and nuances of the African family experience. We have discovered that deep, enduring families are founded on clear communication and mutual respect—and shared values—supporting cultural traditions and adapting to contemporary realities.

In this book, we've explored how to cultivate our marriage, how to raise our children with intention, and how to navigate the tangled web of extended family relationships. We've dealt with some of the most common obstacles: managing finances; conflict and anger resolution; fostering intimacy—even when society is against you. By discussing these topics, we learned so much about how to create a home environment where there is love, growth, and resilience.

Family life is a dynamic process that demands my undivided attention, patience, and love. There is no single right way to live as a family, as we've seen, nor may there be among the myriad of African cultures. However, families can find their own rhythm working together to create harmony at home using the principles and strategies outlined in this book.

Family harmony is not about perfection but about progress and perseverance. This is about building an environment in which each family member feels appreciated, listened to, and loved. By doing so, you can build robust relationships, savor your culture, and acclimatize to the evolving cosmos encircling you. Doing so will help you be ready for the challenges life may throw while creating a life with a united family that can overcome any obstacle that comes your way.

Therefore, let the learnings of these pages inspire your journey towards peace at home. May you continue to love and forgive one another; may your love grow stronger and deeper each day. So, as you apply these 10 strategies and principles, know that achieving harmony at home is not just a goal but a wonderful journey, filled with friendships and possibilities that you and your loved ones embark on together.

Don't miss out!

Visit the website below and you can sign up to receive emails whenever Stanley Mwadzama publishes a new book. There's no charge and no obligation.

https://books2read.com/r/B-A-BEJAD-QXPLF

BOOKS 2 READ

Connecting independent readers to independent writers.

About the Author

Stanley Mwadzama is an African author and storyteller who is passionate about upholding and disseminating the principles that characterize African families. He was inspired to address the universal issues that families face in the modern world by his own cultural background and experiences, having been born and raised in Malawi. When Stanley was in high school, he began writing and contributed to the school newspaper. *Harmony at Home: A Guide to African Family Life* is his first book.

He is committed to fostering closer family ties and highlighting the value of communication, comprehension, and tradition in his roles as a husband and father.

When Stanley is not writing, he likes to watch movies and spend time with his family.

www.ingramcontent.com/pod-product-compliance
Lightning Source LLC
LaVergne TN
LVHW052050160826
845678LV00015B/3159